Let's Climax Together: The Power of Perseverance

Let's Climax Together, Volume 1

Dr. Michael A. Smith

Published by Dr. Michael A. Smith, 2024.

While every precaution has been taken in the preparation of this book, the publisher assumes no responsibility for errors or omissions, or for damages resulting from the use of the information contained herein.

LET'S CLIMAX TOGETHER: THE POWER OF PERSEVERANCE

First edition. October 22, 2024.

Copyright © 2024 Dr. Michael A. Smith.

ISBN: 979-8224304219

Written by Dr. Michael A. Smith.

Table of Contents

Let's Climax Together!...1

Dedication 4

Acknowledgment 5

About the Author..7

Preface..11

Introduction: First Steps beyond the Ordinary 12

Chapter One: Grit under the Microscope 17

Chapter 2: Breaking Barriers...29

Chapter 3: Allies on the Climb 34

Chapter 4: Habitual Heroes...40

Chapter 5: Failures to Frontiers..45

Chapter 6: Summiting Your Everest 51

Let's Climax Together!

The Power of Perseverance

"Our greatest glory is not in never falling, but in rising every time we fall."
– Confucius

LET'S CLIMAX TOGETHER: THE POWER OF PERSEVERANCE3

Dedication

I dedicate this series to Special Education students, kids with ADHD, veterans suffering from mental health conditions, people fighting addictions, college dropouts, those who feel stifled and limited, and the gifted, talented, but often undervalued individuals seeking new horizons.

This dedication goes out to the oppressed, the marginalized, the "counted out," and those who were told they would never amount to anything in life!

I also dedicate this to the late bloomers, entrepreneurs, CEOs, Managers, Blue-Collar Workers, university students, dreamers, and those who want to reach for the stars.

Go for it! Grab life by the horns! Never Give Up! Keep Climbing & Let's Climax Together!

Acknowledgment

I want to take a moment to express my heartfelt gratitude to everyone who contributed to the creation of the "**Let's Climax Together**" 7-book series, beginning with this first book: **The Power of Perseverance**. This journey has been challenging and rewarding, and I could not have completed it without the support of many extraordinary individuals.

First and foremost, I want to thank my family and friends for their unwavering encouragement and belief in me. Your constant motivation and patience inspired me through the most challenging moments of this writing journey.

To Dr. Lance and Lora Shand, your steadfast support and prayers made all the difference, reminding me daily of the importance of perseverance in our lives. I am saddened today, just a few days after my 48th birthday, to be grieving the passing of Dr. Shand, my undergraduate studies religion and theology professor. I lift up Momma Shand, Lola Shand, and the entire family in prayer.

I sincerely thank my mentors and coaches for their invaluable guidance and wisdom. Your teachings have deepened my understanding of perseverance and sparked my passion for sharing these lessons with others. I especially want to acknowledge Ms. Robin Risolo, my grammar school teacher, who believed in me and illuminated a dark time in my childhood. I am also grateful to Dr. John Ramos, my high school principal, who served as a father figure during my father's incarceration. Your leadership, patience, and example have profoundly influenced my life's journey, ultimately helping me achieve my doctoral degree.

I know countless individuals have supported me, and I regret that I might not be able to mention everyone without unintentionally overlooking someone. However, I do want to take a moment to recognize a few incredible people who have stood by me since "day one": Regina, the Richardsons, the Woolcocks, the Shands, the late Dean Philip Nixon, the late Aunt Ella-Mae, the late Aunt Ruth, Aunt Gwen

Feathers, the Lockett's, the Edmonds, the McCracken's, and my brothers from Phi Beta Sigma Fraternity, Incorporated.

Lastly, I owe particular gratitude to Minister Frederick A. Whitlow II, DHL (h.c.), whose support was instrumental in my recovery after my stroke; I genuinely owe my life to him.

Finally, I extend my thanks to you, the reader. Your willingness to embark on this journey with me is the ultimate motivation. I hope the insights within these pages resonate with your experiences and inspire you to embrace your full potential. Together, let's strive for success and celebrate every step of the journey.

Thank you for being a part of this adventure! With appreciation and hope, Let's Climax Together!

— Dr. Mike

About the Author

Dr. Michael Smith hails from the beautiful island nation of **Jamaica.** He spent his formative years in Norwalk, Connecticut, after immigrating at a young age. It was there that the **Norwalk SDA Church** recognized and confirmed his call to ministry at the age of 12. After completing high school, Dr. Smith enlisted in the **United States Navy,** where he began his ministry as a **Chaplain's Assistant.** He was ordained as a Deacon at 19 and later into the Gospel Ministry at 21. After four years of active duty, he felt the call to pursue formal academic ministerial training.

Dr. Smith relocated to Huntsville, AL, where he enrolled at Oakwood University, majoring in Ministerial Theology. While at Oakwood, he also in the **Alabama Army National Guard** as a **Combat Military Police Officer.** After completing his studies at Oakwood, he continued in ministry, serving in various leadership, academic, corporate, and community roles over the past 30 years.

Dr. Smith holds a **Doctor of Healthcare Administration** from Virginia University of Lynchburg. He is a **PsyD(c) at the American International Theism University.** He also earned an **MBA, a Master of Project Management, a Master of Human Resources Management, and a Master of Business and Corporate Communications** from Universidad Isabel I in Barcelona, Spain. Additionally, he is pursuing a **Master of Arts in Human Rights Practice** at the University of Arizona. Dr. Smith is a **Fellow of the Institute of Management Consultants - Nigeria** and a **Certified Management Consultant (CMC®).**

Furthermore, Dr. Smith is a **National Mental Health First Aid Instructor** with the National Council for Mental Wellbeing and a **Certified ACT Therapist.** He is also a **Certified DEIB Expert** with a **Diversity, Equity, Inclusion, and Belonging in the Workplace Certification** from the Muma College of Business at the University of South Florida. His additional qualifications include expertise in **Enterprise Risk Management/FMEA,** service as a **Human Rights**

Consultant with the U.S. Institute of Diplomacy and Human Rights, and **Certification as a Professional Grant Writer** with The Grantsmanship Center.

Currently, Dr. Smith serves as an **Adjunct Professor** at **Universidad Isabel I / [ENEB] European Business School of Barcelona,** where he teaches several Masters-level courses. He is the former **Chapter Chaplain** of the **Nu Nu Sigma Chapter** of **Phi Beta Sigma Fraternity, Inc.** He also previously served as the **New Mexico State Director** of **Bigger & Better Business.**

Dr. Smith is the President and CEO of **Phoenix Risk Management & Consulting Firm, LLC.**

Through his vast array of experiences and accomplishments, coupled with his personal struggles with Sexual Addiction, Depression, Anxiety, Child Domestic Violence Survivor, and Stroke Survivor, Dr. Smith continues to inspire and influence others to reach their full potential, He stands as a beacon of success and inspiration in today's ever-evolving world.

His hobbies include Scenic Photography, DIY Candle-making, Astronomy, and Co-Hosting the No More Dirty Radio Show in Huntsville, AL.

LET'S CLIMAX TOGETHER: THE POWER OF PERSEVERANCE9

Page Blank Intentionally

Preface

The journey toward fulfillment often feels daunting in a world filled with challenges, setbacks, and uncertainties. Many of us find ourselves at a crossroads, facing obstacles that seem insurmountable. In these moments, we must remember the true essence of our potential—the power of perseverance.

"Let's Climax Together! The Power of Perseverance" is not merely a book; it's an invitation to embark on an empowering journey that transcends personal struggles. In these pages, you will discover that perseverance is not just a trait to admire in others—it's a skill that can be developed and harnessed within each of us. My goal is to share my experiences, struggles, and the stories of those who inspire us with their resilience.

Through heartfelt anecdotes, practical strategies, and relatable insights, this book offers a roadmap for navigating life's hurdles and achieving our dreams. In every chapter, I hope to shine a light on the triumph of the human spirit—reminding you that setbacks are not the end but stepping stones toward your greatest achievements.

As you journey through these words, I urge you to reflect on your experiences and obstacles. Embrace the idea that perseverance is not about never failing; it is about rising each time we fall and pushing forward with renewed determination. Together, we will explore the transformative power of resilience and learn to celebrate every triumph, no matter how small.

Let's embark on this journey together. Let's reignite our passions, fortify our spirits, and inspire one another to reach our highest potential. Remember, the climb may be steep, but we can reach the summit together.

Welcome to "Let's Climax Together!"—a celebration of perseverance and its incredible power to transform our lives.

Introduction: First Steps beyond the Ordinary

"I am struggling to stay committed! I can't persevere anymore!" a person in agony wallows.
"Oh, you know how the saying goes: if at first, you don't succeed, try again!"

We've all encountered this clichéd catchphrase at various points in our lives. For example, when life heaps all its challenges and burdens upon us, leaving us feeling trapped and hopeless, a familiar voice may echo in our minds, repeating this overused phrase to soothe us. But does it help? It usually doesn't, for human nature is the hobgoblin of consistency. We yearn for it, yet it seems so far out of reach. And once we commit, the hardships along our path plague our minds with the desire to give up.

"Neither am I a child nor a robot who will take this quote at face value. Success is not guaranteed by hindsight; I need something much more motivating to push me forward."

A similar reply might be bogged down on the face of the comforter because, frankly speaking, we are tired of hearing it. Tired of constantly being let down by reality. Tired of rebuilding the blocks of life only for them to be broken down by unfortunate circumstances. We become overwhelmed and confused, losing ourselves in the process. Even after identifying the issue, with our lives at a standstill, we cling to old habits that may be destructive. If we can't solve a math equation, we resort to cheating our way to the answer. If we can't lose weight efficiently, we fall into yo-yo dieting or binge eating to cope. Impatience is the root cause of many problems. When our journey toward self-improvement pauses, it aggravates us, leading us to take shortcuts that set us further back than where we started, ultimately demotivating us from trying again. There may be a whole sea of paths waiting for us to explore, yet we seem to stick to the familiar square, paradoxically feeling the urge to move forward while remaining stuck.

Such is the unfortunate slump that many of us face. Our hopelessness in these situations makes sense. But what is also sensible is believing that there is a way out. There are ways to renavigate, relocate, or even change the entire premise of our journey. But all of this can only be done through one source, and one source only: *perseverance.*

Take the example of Walt Disney, who was once surrounded by rejections of his artistic ventures. Struggling with financial issues and the fear of uncertainty, he could have given up. But he powered through, pushed his limits, and tested them with patience and perhaps a positive outlook on life. Through consistency and steadfast dedication to his vision, he built an infinite empire that continues to spark joy in people's lives. Perseverance helped him overcome his hardships.

Perseverance is a commitment and determination to achieve a goal, regardless of its enormity. It is like an alarm clock in one's head that goes off when demotivation clouds our minds. It brings us back to our initial reason for mustering the courage to pursue a particular task. Through perseverance, we are reminded to do the right thing, a powerful force that steers us in the proper direction of our reality. It is the golden key to unlocking one's highest potential. It is a tool that has been employed since the dawn of humanity. Take, for example, Greek heroes like Sisyphus and Achilles from the tragedies of Homer and Virgil. The heroes created in these poets' worlds were determined to reach their goals, even if it meant their demise. Possessed with determination and strong will, they fought fiercely, their eyes always fixed on the prize.

"Let me not then die ingloriously and without a struggle, but let me first do some great thing that shall be told among men hereafter."
– Homer, The Iliad

Despite life-altering or fatal consequences, these heroes stayed true to their causes and goals, achieving immortality in their names. Contemporary people admire their fearlessness and dedication.

Perseverance flows through every vein of humanity, gathering all of man's courage and revealing a mirage of the goal that first inspired him. It is essential to provide a reason for a man to wake up each day and push forward, enduring significant hardships to survive as someone who knows he has made a difference in his own life and/or in the lives of others.

This first of seven books delves into the subject of perseverance. It examines persistence and how one can rely on it to achieve their goals. It's important to remember that every expert in a field was once a beginner, a learner who faced confusion, fear of failure, and demotivation. Though challenging, overcoming internal demons to fulfill your dreams is achievable when you understand the importance of perseverance. Time may be man's worst enemy, but not when you're on a journey toward your goals. It is always possible to gather the motivational pieces that perseverance offers and solve the puzzle of life. While some may find perseverance natural, others might not know where to begin.

This book is divided into six chapters or phases that explore perseverance and the pieces of our goals, which must be joined together. First, perseverance will be broken down to reveal the backbones that give it form: grit, resilience, and tenacity. These elements fuel the passion for a goal and drive you toward it. Grit embodies strength and integrity, which are the driving forces behind perseverance. Resilience and tenacity follow as key attributes in performing tasks that affirm your goals. This explanation is supported by stories from the past–tales that preserve the importance of perseverance.

At times, we find ourselves burned out, with no answers to the ever-growing questions about the future of our goals and challenges. It feels as if the world has ended. That's when a small spark of hope ignites, motivating us to persevere. As Rachel Scott said,

"Perseverance is the act of continuing to move forward, even when you want to give up."

Everyone makes mistakes, setbacks are inevitable, and failure often accompanies complex processes. But the result of achieving goals is worth the wait and the pain. This is where the next helping hand of this book comes in, guiding you through hard times with perseverance.

Perseverance also proves valuable when you need a boost in confidence, lifting you from the depths of fear and insecurity. It jolts you into action, where fear is replaced by trial and practice. Consistency in effort is key, and it can only be maintained through perseverance.

In addition to internal strength, external support is crucial. The core chapters focus on exploring support groups and motivational influences that shape our daily lives. Surrounding yourself with people who have faced similar struggles and are either working toward or have achieved their goals can push you closer to your own happiness. As rightly observed, *"Never before have humans been so aware of one another's struggles, pain, and perseverance."* This heightened awareness, brought about by our interconnected world, unites us in our struggles. Growth in unity should always be encouraged. As existentialists believe, ***"We are all in this together."*** Every day, we create individual meanings for our lives, and we see our surroundings reflect our efforts.

Perseverance is a continuous process, an exploration of our personality, and a journey toward contentment. Devotion to a cause that holds true meaning in your life is essential for reaching limitless possibilities.

Reversing a downward spiral has always been humanity's struggle. We need to recognize ourselves as worthy of the lives we've been blessed with and breathe the air of a proud person. Yet, something gnaws at us—anxiety that stalls our progress toward betterment. In the fast-paced world we live in, we can exhaust ourselves with overthinking rather than acting on our goals. When asked, "Why didn't you accomplish such-and-such task?" we are often left blank, knowing the fault lies within our self-destructive cycles. Now, more than ever, it's time to get started.

Getting started, no matter how small or underwhelming the beginning might seem, is the most crucial step in overcoming self-inflicted setbacks. While the world rushes past, we need to steady ourselves, pushing forward with each step. We must let the uncertainty of the future settle and continue striving for a better tomorrow, hoping for the best. The universe always responds, in one way or another.

Consistency becomes more accessible to commit to when perseverance is excluded from the equation. Perseverance pushed Marie Curie to break through gender barriers and embark on her scientific journeys. It inspired William Golding to continue publishing his novel The Lord of the Flies after being rejected numerous times. Perseverance has been shown to save the lives of individuals trapped in a vast abyss of depression and fear of failure. It also lingered on the island where Chuck Noland, from Cast Away, found himself stranded, pushing him to get up every single day and live his life despite the uncertainty of being saved. It can also be found in the deepest oceans, where Nemo's father, Marlin, frantically searched for his son, with only hope and perseverance by his side to give him the courage to keep looking.

Now, the phrase, "if you fail, try, try again," carries a bit of depth. This book will explore this sentiment, unraveling its nature and highlighting the importance of perseverance and how man clings to it like wet sand on empty shells.

Chapter 1: Grit under the Microscope

I recall a vivid memory of a man surrounded by the underlying issues of his past and hardships due to his distorted mental health, struggling to become a high achiever yet surrounded by people who were stuck on land. At the same time, he wanted to soar high in the sky. He had leadership potential but was enclosed in a space where freedom could never flourish.

The man is me. Most individuals reading this book, including myself, have dealt with at least one of these challenges in their lives. These challenges could manifest as obstacles, setbacks, or the forced numbness we experience after being bombarded with voices that don't believe in our dreams. Often, we find ourselves surrounded by negativity, where those around us attempt to bury our aspirations in places so deep that we lose sight of them. Our dreams, the essence of our hope and ambition, become distant, clouded by the doubt instilled by others. To reclaim that ambition, to reignite the fire that fuels our capabilities, we need a key—a key to unlock the door that's been shut by those destructive thoughts. That key can be found in no other place than in the powerful semblance of perseverance.

Perseverance is a force that cannot be overstated. It is built upon three key pillars: grit, resilience, and tenacity. These pillars are not just abstract concepts—they form the foundation upon which perseverance stands and extend its boundaries into every aspect of our lives. Whether in our professional pursuits or personal growth, these elements intertwine to create the driving force that pushes us beyond our perceived limits.

Let's revisit the shadows cast upon dreamers by nonbelievers, those who attempt to extinguish the light within us. It is entirely plausible that these forces of demotivation will, at times, hit us with such intensity that we fail to see the next step on our path. This is when the true essence of perseverance must rise to the forefront. The key features that build perseverance—grit, resilience, and tenacity—become essential tools for survival and progress. Grit, in particular, is the unwavering commitment to a goal, regardless of how long-term or distant that goal may seem.

Consider the case of a man trying to quit smoking. For a time, he may experience significant hardships—cravings, physical discomfort, moments of doubt—all of which may feel like barriers too large to overcome. However, if he remains consistent, steadfast in his goal, he will immerse himself in the experience of achieving something greater than mere short-term relief. He will encounter setbacks; it's inevitable. But perseverance, especially the grit to keep pushing forward, allows him to stay on course, fighting for something more profound than the temporary satisfaction of giving up.

Now, imagine another man standing at a different kind of crossroads, facing hurdles in his career. Perhaps he finds himself unable to secure the job he desires, or he lacks the proper tools to progress financially, leaving him feeling insecure in his role. Worse still, he might be contemplating a complete career shift, hoping that by doing so, he will find greater happiness, but he hesitates. He hesitates because of the fear of the unknown, the risks that come with change. What can help him navigate this uncertainty? Grit. That unyielding drive to pursue his aspirations. Through grit, he finds a glimmer of light, a path to follow when the road ahead feels shrouded in doubt. Through it, he uncovers the confidence to push forward, to advocate for himself, and to strive for the betterment of his life.

Resilience, another critical pillar of perseverance, is the ability to recover from setbacks. It's the bounce-back factor—the mindset that, regardless of how many times we fall, we rise again, each time with a little more wisdom, a little more strength. The man who quit smoking? He might stumble, have moments of weakness, but resilience pulls him back onto the path. The man uncertain about his career? He may face rejection, or the fear of failure may temporarily paralyze him, but with resilience, he's able to dust himself off and keep moving forward, unafraid of trying again and again.

Then, there's tenacity. It's the pillar that fortifies the first two. Tenacity is what keeps us pushing, long after others might have given up. It's the relentless pursuit of our goals, not just in the face of adversity, but in the face of monotony and weariness. When progress feels slow, when rewards seem distant, tenacity is what drives us forward, step by step.

The man is me, but the man is also you, and anyone who has faced obstacles that feel too large, too painful, or too exhausting to overcome. Perseverance is not a quality reserved for the fortunate or the extraordinary; it's a skill, a mindset, which anyone can cultivate. It is the key to unlocking doors that others have closed on our behalf, and it is the force that allows us to rise, time and again, toward our greatest potential.

We all face our own mountains. But whether those mountains are built by external forces—like the discouragement of others—or by our own self-doubt, the principles of perseverance remain the same. Grit, resilience, and tenacity will help us climb, even when the summit seems impossibly far away.

So, as you continue through these pages, take a moment to reflect on your own journey. Think about the challenges you've faced, the doubts that have clouded your path, and the setbacks that have made you question your dreams. Then, ask yourself: What will it take to keep moving forward? How can you harness the power of perseverance in your own life? Together, we will explore these questions, and together, we will find the strength to rise, again and again, until we reach the summit.

Because that's what perseverance is—it's not about never failing. It's about rising each time we fall, with renewed determination and an unshakable belief in our potential. It's about understanding that the climb is steep, yes, but the summit is always within reach if we keep going.

The man is me. But the man can also be you.

"Easier said than done!"

From the introduction, the man might chime in to express his skepticism towards such beliefs, which is indeed as easy as it sounds.

Finding grit is like uncovering the last few missing pieces of a puzzle. It requires enough navigational effort to push you toward a self-discovery of such importance that it might leave you in disbelief. Grit, as a motivational tool, paradoxically resides inside you. While it can be hard to bring it out due to our overbearing self-doubt and insecurities, once it sits comfortably at the forefront of our minds, it can help us overcome all our problems. To make this easier, let's imagine it as a pearl jammed inside a clam. To yank it out, you need some tools to assist you in the job. A pair of clippers or even some tweezers could do the trick.

Similarly, to bring the pearl out of the void of our conscience, we need the assistance of tools like self-preservation and self-assurance. Exercises such as talking to yourself, adding motivational quotes, and speaking to yourself in an affirmative tone might bring out Grit and perseverance. Start the day off by looking at your reflection and locking your eyes. Tell yourself, *"I can achieve all my dreams and aspirations. My ability to conquer my fears is abundant, loud enough to shatter all insecurities and self-doubt."*

At first, this might sound silly, especially to those sharing your space. Sooner or later, you'll become comfortable with your reflection and talk to yourself as if conversing with a friend. Treat yourself the way you would want others to treat you. Remember that charity starts with the self, and the self, simmered down in an ocean of insecurities, needs to be pulled back up through positive self-talk and assurance. This is the way out of many hurdles in life because the insecure self can sometimes be the biggest hobgoblin of a motivational and enthusiastic mind.

Now that you have addressed self-talk, the next step toward a more remarkable resilience against setbacks in a productive growth process is writing letters to no one other than yourself! Pick up a pen and paper and write down the things you want to achieve in life, numbering them based on the importance of each particular goal. Then, below that, address your younger self and excuse yourself for the setbacks you have created due to self-doubt and demotivation. This will be a confrontation, addressing all the issues that limit your aspirations.

No matter how smeared your reputation may be, journaling benefits such endeavors. By putting self-intervention aside and passively storing your thoughts in your mind, it will become evident to you where the problem resides and where the barriers and blockages are that stop you from walking your path toward self-assurance and a better life. Straightforward navigation adds a significant step to the process. Additionally, minor setbacks can cloud your clarity, which is where Grit, veiled in the deep layers of perseverance, assists you, just as it did initially.

Setbacks also need the support of the second pillar of perseverance: resilience. Resilience is the ability to prevent yourself from withdrawing from progress due to setbacks. Consider it like the water bottle handlers during marathon races. They wait for each contestant at specific points along the race route to assist the runners with their disqualifying and intense thirst. Resilience is the strength that can be cultivated through the previously mentioned suggestions. Consistent self-talk, rereading your confrontation letters, and working on another letter to state your progress–addressed to your younger self–are all beneficial. Dedicating letters to the vision of your childhood will provide motivation and a valid reason to support your progress and achievements. Building the strength to overlook setbacks and demotivational incidents takes time and effort. For such negatives, counteracting them with coping mechanisms is always a plausible solution. Exercises like yoga, jogging, working out, being consistent with therapy, and surrounding yourself with positive influences can help counteract the issues and hurdles you face in your tasks. Having resilience, therefore, creates a firm hold on perseverance as well.

Tenacity contributes to the development of the habit of perseverance. Being tenacious leads to the accomplishment of the goals you've set for yourself. This rigidity allows you to stick to your beliefs without letting the opinions of others cloud your mind. Self-contentment also results from being tenacious. As D.H. Lawrence notes when he addresses our national poet's work, Walt Whitman, each soul has a different path, and it doesn't interrupt the road of other souls who walk alongside but on entirely different paths toward various destinations.

In certain instances, tenacity can be mistaken for stubbornness due to the firmness of one's opinions. However, clinging to one's beliefs and working toward one's destined achievements differs from falling into the yo-yo pit of being recognized as stubborn. Some hardships come along with the desire for accomplishments and success in life. Persistence, and ultimately perseverance, made up of tenacity, broaden our horizons and increase our experience and knowledge.

Tenacity is a mature form of resilience that helps us see through all surface-level criticism, whether from ourselves or others. As mentioned, it uplifts dreamers to hover in the skies that belong to them, while letting the critics and doubters fall back to the ground to sulk in awe and wonder. Tenacity is consistency at its most ruthless and awe-inspiring extreme. It is the secret to all kinds of success, each with its own unique backstory. As Louis Pasteur said, *"Let me tell you the secret that has led me to my goal. My strength lies solely in my tenacity."*

If you examine perseverance closely, you'll discover that it's made up of small but powerful elements, the most essential of which is grit. This consistency of effort demands an unwavering combination of positivity, self-assurance, resilience, tenacity, and confidence. Together, these qualities create a foundation for success, allowing a person to approach each new day as an opportunity for growth and conquest, no matter the challenges that lie ahead.

Now, picture the somber image of a broken man, tied to the destructive strings of his childhood. It's a painful scene, but there's also a glimmer of hope—a belief that the potential for perseverance, and eventual success, is within his grasp. In truth, this broken man could be anyone, because the journey of perseverance doesn't belong to just one person. It's a universal experience, and, like so many young people, I once found myself in a similar situation.

I was often seen as a person with leadership qualities, someone with great potential. Growing up, I was an inquisitive and creative student, constantly asking questions, always willing to voice my concerns and challenge the status quo. But life's inevitable hurdles followed me closely, like a shadow, waiting for the right moment to strike. And when they did, it was with the ferocity of a predator, devouring the positivity I had fought to hold on to.

I was diagnosed with ADHD early on and placed in special education classes. This immediately changed the trajectory of my education, leading to poor grades and a growing sense of anxiety about my future. I didn't come from privilege; my upbringing was far from stable. I was adopted as an infant, relocated from Jamaica to the United States, where I entered a new world of confusion and hardship. My adoptive parents were drug dealers, and my home environment was marked by abuse and instability.

To add to the chaos, I lost out on the chance to build a bond with my father. He was incarcerated throughout my formative years, missing from my life during the period I needed him most—my high school years. I was a confused and heartbroken teenager, grappling with the sense of loss and insecurity that came with his absence. Demotivation was like a train wreck, hurtling toward me at full speed, building over time until it felt like I had nowhere left to turn.

In those years, I was consumed by doubt and insecurity. I questioned my worth, my ability to succeed, and even my capacity to survive in a world that felt indifferent to my struggles. But in retrospect, I realize that those very years of hardship—those moments of darkness—were the incubators for the perseverance that would eventually rise within me.

Just as perseverance is built from the core elements of grit, it is also forged in the fires of adversity. It doesn't emerge when life is easy; it's born from the struggle. And while the pain of my early life threatened to derail me, it was perseverance that ultimately helped me survive and even thrive in the face of those challenges.

What's the point of living such a life? Full of brutal uncertainties, a ruthless present, and a traumatic past?

It took me years to fully grasp perseverance, but once I did, my gradual efforts began to manifest in tangible ways. My story, which will unfold throughout this book, serves as an example that even those with the most difficult childhoods can become successful and motivated individuals. The three keys, when combined with patience, allow perseverance to blossom in our lives. Life isn't easy; it can cripple us and leave us feeling distorted and demotivated, drained of any ambition. Life throws obstacles our way when we are trying to muster the little strength we have left. But there is always a spark amidst the void, a tiny glimmer of hope, like *"matches struck unexpectedly in the dark,"* as Virginia Woolf once said.

Both our professional and personal lives need the support of perseverance. No matter how small the task may seem, staying consistent pushes us out of our slumps and back to work. Take, for example, a struggling actor who continually attends auditions, only to face rejection time and again. Despite his persistent efforts, he fails to recognize his potential and is left to brood over his worries about achieving greatness. This is where the previously mentioned tools become valuable. Among them, perseverance stands out as the vital force within him, waiting to be ignited. It will empower him to keep seeking audition opportunities, maintain his belief in himself, and radiate the confidence others admire. These qualities will propel him toward success and fulfillment, ultimately leading him to prosperity.

Take, for example, a case from personal life: personal growth that makes us better people. A man troubled by morbid obesity finds himself haunted by his food addiction. For the sake of his health, he needs to lose weight. It is a daily struggle to wake up and resist the urge to binge excessively, yet he does it because the promise of a solid reward keeps him focused. Healthy weight loss requires consistency and time, and only a person with remarkable resilience can achieve it. This man, with great resilience, commits to his weight loss journey. Slowly but surely, he becomes the healthy man he aspired to be. It is perseverance–and perseverance alone–that drives progress.

Such personal and professional examples are common, appearing in the experiences of every person. The patience and perseverance required to overcome challenges lift us out of negative whirlpools. These whirlpools can affect personal relationships as well. Miscommunication and misunderstandings may limit contact with friends and family, but with perseverance, one can resist the urge to retaliate harshly. Patience and perseverance are the keys to overcoming all public, private, or academic obstacles.

Serena Williams, a four-time Olympic gold medalist, is a symbol of perseverance. When asked what she is most proud of, she replied:

"I'm most proud of just being able to persevere. I think perseverance is something that should be talked about more. Staying in it through the negatives and positives, and still having a career that spans over two decades, is pretty awesome. And I'm really fortunate that I've been able to do that."

Perseverance carried her through injuries and challenges on the tennis court. Though she was ranked No. 1 in singles by the *Women's Tennis Association*, her proudest moment pays tribute to her perseverance. Like anyone else, she stood firm in the face of adversity, relying on perseverance during her darkest times. Self-belief, confidence, and resilience push great individuals like her to achieve miraculous things in life. It takes just one person to change the course of your life: you.

Similarly, from ages ago, we have the example of Elvis Presley, an adored musician and performer, who was once told by his manager:

"You ain't goin' nowhere, son. You ought to go back to driving a truck."

This musical legend, known for his iconic dance moves and unforgettable performances, faced rejection early on. But the power of perseverance strengthened his confidence on stage and in his music, eventually making him the icon of the 1970s.

Looking even further back in history, we have the invention of the Wright Brothers' airplane. Today, the idea of flying seems normal, but long ago, when people only knew how to travel by land and sea, the concept of flying was utterly foreign. As Wilbur Wright once said:

"I confess that I told my brother Orville that man would not fly for fifty years."

But through failure, they pushed on, showing resilience and proving themselves to be achievers. Attempting to take flight and crashing, time and again, they persevered because they had the self-assurance that comes with perseverance. As it's said:

"It is not necessary to hope to persevere."

Their initial skepticism of their own success was understandable, but they overcame it.

Examples like these are abundant in the pages of history and in our present, showcasing the incredible capacity of humans to achieve greatness through the simple act of perseverance.

It's important to note, however, that stubbornness and perseverance are two very different things. While stubbornness and excessive rigidity can lead to setbacks, perseverance fosters growth and progress. To illustrate, consider a mouse that goes to the mousetrap every night to get the cheese. It knows the danger, but its stubbornness could be fatal. Even though the mouse could find cheese in the pantry or a dumpster, it repeatedly returns to the trap, risking its life. This reflects how destructive habits can ruin a person's progress. If a puzzle piece doesn't fit, you shouldn't force it. Instead, look for another piece, adjust your approach, and minimize setbacks.

Thus, perseverance is built on three pillars: tenacity, resilience, and Grit. This foundation must be firmly established in everyone's life, including mine.

Now, imagine you're sitting in your childhood room, confronted by your younger self. What would you tell yourself about your successes, setbacks, and challenges? How do you think your younger self would react?

Chapter 2: Breaking Barriers

A gym fanatic once found himself stuck indoors as a downpour ruined his plans for leg day. He had set goals for himself, jotting down the number of squats and lunges he planned to achieve that day. But the sudden rain blocked the streets, making it impossible for him to get to the gym. A puddle in the way (literally!) disrupted his routine. Now, there are two ways he could handle this unexpected turn of events: he could either accept defeat or mope around the house, seeing this minor setback as a failure, or he could view the rain as a blessing, with his garden getting watered without him needing to lift a finger. He could do his exercises at home, enjoying his time indoors. The latter option is grounded in the theory of **Positive Framework.**

This metaphor is a microcosm of how we can view hurdles in our lives. Whether they are minor or major setbacks, sometimes progress doesn't go as planned. When the obstacle is external, it can often be overcome with perseverance, but external limitations, like the rain, are simply forces of nature. These external blocks must be viewed through a positive frame, allowing us to *make the best of things.*

If the gym fanatic in this example finds a way to accommodate his minor setback, he will be better prepared to excel in his goals the next time he visits the gym. Until then, home workouts and relaxing while watching the rain–a reminder from Mother Nature to take a break–may be the best course of action.

Positive frameworks don't just apply to natural setbacks but also to personal limitations. If you find yourself falling into a "pothole" of issues and don't see a way out, it's OK to take a step back, breathe, and rethink your next move. You might realign your goals, look back at your journal to remember why you started pursuing a particular goal in the first place, or simply allow yourself to mess up.

As Edgar Allan Poe famously said, *"find beauty in imperfection."* The beauty of walking a rocky, winding road instead of a straight path to progress is that it has character. It has a story, just like your personality, your face, and your life. Finding joy in minor setbacks helps you truly appreciate the dedication it takes to achieve your goals. Remember that setbacks aren't walls to be stared at; they are walls to climb, to paint murals on, or to decorate with frames that bring joy, rather than agony over limitations.

A recollection of my story might serve as an example of how setbacks can shape our lives in ways we could never anticipate. After enduring years of suffering, battling mental torment, and living within the confines of my own limitations, I finally found a sense of belonging and purpose in academia at the age of 44—a place I had always yearned to be. However, for many years, personal setbacks kept me from pursuing my dreams.

As an adopted child relocated from Jamaica, I often felt like an outsider. My adoptive parents were exposed to lives of drugs, crime, and abuse. As the child of drug dealers, the pleasantries of a typical childhood were out of reach. The dream of a "normal" family life seemed unattainable, leaving me feeling detached from what others took for granted.

Throughout my high school years, mental setbacks compounded the pain of having no paternal influence in my life. My father was incarcerated, and during the crucial period of my adolescence, his absence left a void. Though I managed to graduate high school, I carried the weight of this emptiness with me. I sought refuge by joining the U.S. Navy, where I served for four years, finding a sanctuary and a sense of belonging that had been missing in my life.

Yet, even after my military service, life didn't magically fall into place. Years of homelessness followed. In my twenties, I was a troubled man, wrestling with the aftermath of my past and the uncertainties of my future. As a veteran with only a high school diploma, my job prospects were limited. While I felt the call to ministry, it took over two decades to fully navigate the stress, homelessness, and depression that clung to me.

My mental health struggles gnawed at my spirit, and it often felt like the obstacles were insurmountable. But somehow, through it all, I held on to perseverance, even when it was no more than a flickering candle in the darkest corners of my life.

My personal recollection serves as a reminder that no matter how dense the clouds of despair, there is always a way forward. The experiences I've endured—homelessness, mental health struggles, family trauma—are not definitive. Just as joy is fleeting, so too is sorrow. We cannot guarantee permanence in life's emotional phases, but what we can do is embrace the present moment and trust that everything is working itself out.

Setbacks are inevitable, but they don't have to define us. One way to cope is by fully feeling the moment and allowing the emotions triggered by those setbacks to wash over us. Take a deep breath and let yourself experience frustration, sadness, or anger, without rushing to resolve it. Returning to the example of the gym fanatic who misses a workout or experiences a plateau, a healthy way to deal with that setback is to sit down, allow the frustration to be felt, and then move forward when ready.

Facing the discomfort head-on is an integral part of building perseverance. If anger arises when things don't go as planned, let it. If tears come from failure, let them flow. If doubts cloud your mind and make you question your potential, allow those doubts to surface. But remember, these feelings are temporary—they are like band-aids that fall away when the wound begins to heal. Eventually, you can start again, right from where you left off, and move forward with renewed strength and purpose.

As the saying goes, it's never too late to better yourself. Sometimes, the best way to deal with setbacks is by taking a break. Step away from the situation and relax, reminding yourself that the world isn't out to get you. It's important to understand that time is on your side, and that the turbulent emotions you experience while pursuing your goals are part of the process. This awareness allows you to manage negativity and demotivation more effectively during your journey toward self-improvement.

For example, imagine your goal is to earn an A in all your classes, but due to unforeseen challenges—whether academic, physical, or emotional—you end up with B's instead. Rather than seeing this as a failure, consider it a test of your resilience. Take a step back, engage in activities that bring you joy, and give yourself space to recover. By allowing yourself time to reflect, you can reignite your motivation and approach your goals with a fresh perspective.

Setbacks, no matter how painful, should be met with kindness. In today's fast-paced, competitive world, it's easy to fall victim to false narratives about success. Social media and societal pressures can lead us to believe that everyone else is thriving while we're stuck. But it's essential to remember that someone else's success story doesn't have to be yours. Your path is unique, complete with its own struggles, twists, and turns. And just because your journey isn't linear or picture-perfect, doesn't mean it isn't valuable.

Forgive yourself for the setbacks you encounter. Be kind to yourself when things don't go as planned. Life is full of phases that fluctuate in intensity, feelings, and willpower. Pushing too hard to escape a slump can sometimes backfire, leaving you feeling more stuck than before. Instead, approach your challenges with patience, searching for tools—whether they be support systems, new strategies, or moments of reflection—to help you move forward.

A helpful way to manage these frustrating pauses is by breaking your larger goals into smaller, more achievable ones. For example, if you're trying to quit drinking but feel overwhelmed by social pressure or cravings, start by setting smaller daily goals. By focusing on these incremental successes, you'll build momentum and confidence, gradually chipping away at the larger goal. Each small victory brings you closer to your ultimate objective, without the crushing pressure of perfection.

Perseverance is not about never failing; it's about continuing to rise after every fall. It's about forgiving yourself for imperfections and finding the strength to move forward, one small step at a time. Remember, we are all imperfect beings, and it is through embracing our flaws that we find the true power to persevere.

Sometimes, challenges can't be tackled head-on. As discussed earlier, giving yourself positive self-talk, including daily affirmations, is key to overcoming setbacks.

After taking a break and sitting with uncomfortable feelings, the next step is to analyze the setback. Here are some helpful questions to ask yourself when you feel limited:

1. What triggered the setback?
2. Was my reaction justified?
3. Am I being too hard on myself?
4. How can I avoid future setbacks?
5. What changes can I make to my approach to ensure long-term progress?

See your obstacles as stepping stones—a chance to pause and reflect on your progress, no matter how small, and continue moving forward. Even a tiny step forward is a significant accomplishment and something to celebrate. It will motivate you to persevere.

Imagine you are your own coach, dealing with a client (yourself) who is stuck in a slump. What words of advice and encouragement would you offer to help them push through and continue their progress?

Chapter 3: Allies on the Climb

Birds of a feather flock together.

When introducing ourselves to new people with similar interests, we often use this cliché to draw them towards us. Communities of friends form in areas of shared interest. Our social surroundings are made up of people who are similar to us. We tend to influence them, and they, in turn, influence us.

That is why it is essential to surround yourself with positive people. While certain personality traits and characteristics align with those of our friends, some differences can create boundaries between us. These boundaries can lead to potentially issues, so it's important to assess how problematic those differences might be. Some may clash over political views or philosophical debates, while others might face moral conflicts. Specific ethical issues, such as differing ideas of support and help, can negatively impact our lives if not aligned.

For example, a man struggling with work-life balance might ask his friend for advice but receive a demotivating response that only deepens his problem. Responses like, *"That's just how life is"* or *"Sometimes, you just have to give in"* can have damaging.

This is where supportive groups come in. Having a positive friend or two in your life can bring about significant changes. Think of a puppy, tired of chasing its tail and living alone. The excitement and improvement in its mood would skyrocket if it were to have a companion. It's the same with plants–a seed sprouts into a plant and eventually grows into a tree. Like plants, humans have this trait too. Having a friend, whether in a partner or family member, can transform your life.

The next best thing is having the *right kind of friends*–those who are there for you when you need them, those who help and support you. For instance, a man struggling to lift his target weight of the day might push through if he has supportive friends cheering him on. Simple words of encouragement like *"You can do it"* and *"You've got this"* can work wonders. Motivation often stems from affirmation, and while self-affirmation is crucial, hearing it from others can be just as powerful.

Perseverance and success come from hard work, but external support can make the journey easier. Humans are social creatures; we need others around us to feel safe and valued. When it comes to personal growth, seeking help is perfectly normal. Perseverance isn't a solitary journey. Though we may be individuals, we are united by common experiences.

As mentioned earlier, the path to progress is rarely smooth. Challenges may block the way, and we often need a helping hand to overcome them.

"No man is an island, entire of itself; every man is a piece of the continent, a part of the main." – John Donne.

We are all connected through our differences, and within these differences lie the potential for shared struggles and mutual support. The journey toward success, fulfillment, or any significant goal often requires leaning on others, finding common ground, and embracing those differences as points of connection. This sense of connection isn't only limited to the people we meet, but also the environments we find ourselves in. Supportive spaces—whether they be libraries, serene coffee shops, or peaceful parks—can have an immense impact on our ability to reflect and stay focused on the work ahead. These environments act like safe havens, providing the necessary pause that allows us to regroup, reflect, and keep moving forward. In contrast, chaotic or overstimulating spaces can drain our energy and hinder our progress.

Like a carefully tended garden, humans need regular check-ins, whether through self-care, structured support, or professional help. It's important to acknowledge that not every problem can be solved alone or with the help of friends and family. There are moments when professional assistance becomes not just an option but a necessity. For example, individuals struggling with addiction might seek help through organizations like Alcoholics Anonymous, while students wrestling with academic pressures might benefit from tutors. These interventions aren't signs of weakness; rather, they signify a commitment to growth. Reaching out for help enhances your progress, propelling you toward your goals in ways that self-reliance alone might not.

The type of professional help can vary greatly, ranging from in-person therapy sessions to online communities and mentorship programs. Seeking out these avenues of assistance is a reflection of strength, not weakness. In fact, working with a mentor or therapist can help you uncover parts of yourself that you didn't even know were there, providing you with fresh perspectives on old problems. But not all therapy has to be directed by someone else—self-directed practices, like journaling, are powerful tools in maintaining mental clarity. Writing down your thoughts, feelings, and challenges can not only relieve stress but also help you crystallize your goals. Journaling is a form of therapy that helps you track progress, celebrate victories, and push through obstacles. It forces you to take a moment of reflection and understand your path more deeply.

As you continue along your journey, celebrating your small wins is essential. Whether it's overcoming a minor challenge or reaching a milestone you've worked hard for, those moments of victory deserve recognition. At the same time, it's equally important to keep your mind and body in balance. Healthcare centers, meditation practices, and community organizations can provide the type of support that extends beyond the physical and into the mental and emotional realms. These resources are vital for individuals who might find themselves struggling, providing the care needed to keep going when things get tough.

One of the best ways to move forward is to adopt qualities from the people you admire. These can be family members, mentors, or even colleagues. By having deep conversations with them and building strong relationships, you can adopt their mindset, habits, and strategies for success. Sometimes, just talking things over with someone you trust is enough to relieve the burden of a problem. Supportive people not only provide a listening ear but also offer constructive feedback that helps you see things from a new angle. Building a network of trusted individuals around you creates a support system that will elevate you when you're feeling stuck.

A collective strategy for pursuing goals is incredibly helpful when the path ahead seems murky or overwhelming. In these times of chaos and uncertainty, leaning on each other becomes crucial. Surrounding yourself with people who lift you up and sharing the burden of your struggles can make even the hardest obstacles more manageable. When you create an environment built on trust and mutual support, you open the door to collaboration and collective problem-solving. Working together helps solve even the most challenging issues and reminds us that, no matter how difficult life gets, we don't have to face it alone.

Let's imagine a scenario where the world is ending. It sounds bleak, but in this situation, everyone knows the end is coming, and they want their last days to be spent in peace and comfort with those they love. Some people might struggle to accept the finality of it, but others will choose to focus on the love and support of their families and friends. They'll spend their last moments close to the people who matter most, providing comfort and strength in the face of the unknown. This imagined scenario reminds us of what truly matters: the people around us. In times of danger or uncertainty, it's the love and support of others that sustains us.

When we find comfort in others, we open ourselves up to their vulnerabilities as well as our own. This shared vulnerability creates a deeper connection, one that can carry us through difficult times. The strength of these connections often becomes apparent during hardship, when we need others the most. Embracing the support of others not only helps us persevere through challenges but also deepens our relationships, making them more meaningful and enduring.

To both give and receive support, there are a few strategies you can use. As we've discussed, friendships and connections are instrumental in helping us persevere. The next step is figuring out ways to better yourself while holding onto these valuable relationships. Holding the ropes of your journey alone can be more difficult than you expect. That's why a collective approach is more effective. When you lean on others, you share the weight of the struggle, making it easier to keep moving forward.

The first and most important strategy is learning to listen—to both others and yourself. Listening isn't just about hearing what others have to say; it's about paying attention to what you might be missing in your own journey. When you're stuck, take a moment to reflect. Look in the mirror, and instead of criticizing yourself, offer words of encouragement. What would you say to a friend who was struggling? Sometimes, offering yourself the same kindness you would give others can break through the mental barriers holding you back. A simple affirmation like "You've got this" can be enough to give you the clarity you need to push forward.

Listening also extends to your role as a friend. When your loved ones are struggling, you can become their shield, protecting them from negativity and offering them a safe space to express their fears and frustrations. Establishing weekly check-ins is a great way to hold each other accountable and make sure everyone stays on track with their goals. These check-ins provide an opportunity to celebrate successes, troubleshoot problems, and offer each other support during difficult times.

We are all unique individuals, and everyone's approach to receiving and giving support will be different. Some people might thrive on pep talks and motivational speeches, while others simply need a listening ear. It's important to respect these differences and tailor your support to meet the needs of those around you. By doing so, you'll create an environment of trust and understanding that fosters growth and resilience. In the end, perseverance isn't something we achieve alone—it's something we build together.

The next step is offering practical help. For example, if your friend needs help staying consistent with the gym, you could offer to go with him. Similarly, if another friend needs help focusing on her studies, you could send her research materials or suggest professional help. Practical support can be incredibly effective, but you must first voice your needs and communicate them clearly. Whether you need physical assistance or emotional support, it's important to express that to others.

This process requires active communication. Find ways to open up about your struggles with your loved ones. Address your issues and offer to help them with theirs. I remember that in my own journey of perseverance, I sought help and never gave up. At 44, when I decided to go back to university, I didn't do it alone. It was the combination of my own willpower and the support I found around me. That support sparked a motivation like a firecracker. With hard work, dedication, and a helping hand or two, I completed my MBA and became the person I am today.

This shows that even though many people may be distant from their struggles, they can come together and find themselves under a shared purpose. Unity within diversity makes us uniquely suited to hold the ropes of life and pull them toward our success.

What is your immediate support system?

If you find yourself in a slump, list some common problems you face and how you would like your support system to help address them.

Chapter 4: Habitual Heroes

"Show up. Dive in. Persevere."

From reading the works of Nietzsche and Morrison and dreaming at his desk at home to becoming the first African American president of the United States, Barack Obama is a figure to remember. His humble attitude, unwavering passion for progress, and reliability brought him to the position he holds in history. The effort, consistency, and love he has for the beauty of life shaped the man he became.

But it wasn't just passion that got him there. Passion without effort is like a corroded piece of silver. It's the power of habit–the Sisyphean tendency to wake up every morning and pull the boulder of your efforts up the mountain, all with a smile on your face.

This doesn't mean you need to start strong or make immediate changes to your life. Small but meaningful adjustments to your daily routine can significantly impact your lifestyle. For instance, beginning your day with a simple routine that includes a refreshing shower and breathing exercises can lead to noticeable improvements.

Research shows that attaching a small change to an already established habit tends to make it last longer. You're more likely to be consistent when you integrate something new into your routine. For example, adding a morning jog to your daily coffee run can make a substantial difference.

One day of jogging instead of taking a cab to get coffee could spark a lifelong habit of early-morning exercise. One forced habit, when attached to a natural one, keeps both in check and tricks the mind into thinking the two habits go hand in hand.

Now that we know this, how do we create the habit of *keeping habits?* Some people struggle with discipline and are too afraid of being labeled weak, so they never try. For such individuals, the FED method can be effective.

What is the FED method? Simply put, it means to Finish what you start, Embrace challenges, and Develop a growth mindset.

First, finish what you start. This doesn't just apply to major milestones in your life but also to everyday routines. For example, finishing a book, making your bed in the morning, completing a personal project, or fixing things around the house. Cultivating this habit eliminates procrastination. It's normal to delay tasks because you feel inadequate or find them intimidating, but procrastination creates a destructive cycle that often stifles talents that should shine. Start small, focusing on minor tasks that give you a sense of achievement and motivate you to tackle larger challenges.

Consider the example of gardening. You bought seeds and were excited to plant vegetables and fruits. But soon, a voice in your head started telling you that gardening is out of your reach–which plants need constant care and that fruits and vegetables require the perfect environment. Eventually, you listen to that voice and abandon the idea altogether.

This might seem like a logical conclusion, but it's not. It's important to remember that the result of your goals shouldn't dominate your thinking; the goal itself should. Even if your plants dry up or don't grow as expected, it doesn't matter because you tried. You invested effort in something you were passionate about, and progress was inevitable. The failure doesn't diminish the hard work–it adds to it. It proves that you are capable of taking a task seriously. Failure cultivates courage; it doesn't suppress it.

Embracing challenges is a critical part of growth. As I mentioned earlier, you must be willing to dive into the unknown, let go of your fears, and immerse yourself in the beauty of the experience. Each challenge you face builds your perseverance, strengthens your character, and hones your abilities. Confidence comes from releasing fear, and success follows when you stop worrying about the consequences of your actions. That being said, it's important not to ignore the potential outcomes of your goals. Instead, let the pursuit of your goal drive your ambition rather than being obsessed with the end result. The journey itself is where you grow, learn, and develop the resilience to handle anything life throws at you.

This naturally leads to the final part of the FED method—developing a growth mindset. When dealing with the demotivating demons in your mind, it's easy to feel like you're fighting an uphill battle every day. Sometimes, even before you begin, the weight of your worries can feel exhausting. But this is precisely the moment when you must push forward. You need to set aside your fear of uncertainty and pursue your goals with persistence. Every challenge you accept strengthens not only your character but also your ability to achieve your ambitions.

Incorporating the FED method into your life—by focusing, embracing challenges, and developing a growth mindset—will boost your confidence and make each step forward feel more manageable. By pushing through obstacles and celebrating the small wins, you can make steady progress. These wins might be as simple as finishing a task you've been avoiding, or even finding joy in moments of calm. It's those little victories that keep the momentum going and make the bigger challenges more approachable.

Another essential factor in progress is self-care. And by self-care, I don't just mean physical care like working out or taking care of your skin. Mental care is just as, if not more, important. Whether it's through therapy, meditation, or even journaling, taking care of your mental health is essential. The mind needs to be healthy to focus on and pursue your goals. Acknowledging your mental and emotional state, and recognizing issues, is the first step toward progress. Once you've identified the areas that need attention, addressing them becomes your next priority.

Mental health, especially, plays a significant role in how we navigate our lives. Depression, for example, can be so debilitating that it drains you of the energy needed to focus on your goals. When your mind is overwhelmed, it can feel like your thoughts are taking over your day, making it impossible to think about anything else. In these situations, seeking help through therapy can be a life-changing decision. Mental health issues are often invisible, and they can wreak havoc on your life before you even realize what's happening. If you've ever found it difficult to get out of bed in the morning, or if you feel like even the smallest tasks are monumental, those could be signs that your mental health needs attention.

Depression affects not only your mind and body but also your spirit. It takes away the light of hope—the flicker that keeps you moving forward. Hope is what drives ambition, and without it, everything seems dark. But this is where therapy and mental health care come in, acting as that light to guide you out of the shadows. Therapy can help you find clarity, allowing your energy, efforts, and abilities to come back into focus, helping you on the road to success.

Growing up, I didn't have a stable home. My parents were caught in an abusive relationship, which left me feeling on edge and trapped in a constant state of instability. When you're raised in an environment like that, there's little room for ambition. My mind was consumed with survival, leaving little space for my passions. I'm sharing this to highlight just how crucial mental health is. Without freedom to breathe and recognize my true self, I couldn't fully embrace my capabilities. Overcoming that emotional and psychological turmoil took years.

Mental growth, like all progress, is anything but smooth. It's a process that can take years, and even then, it's ongoing. There's no final destination, but as long as you see improvement, the light of hope will remain alive. For me, reaching middle age brought with it a sense of peace. I returned to school, clearer about my goals than ever before. I realized that the key to success is constant self-improvement. It's about learning from the past while looking forward to the future, building a better version of yourself each day.

Good habits, like journaling, can also be powerful tools for growth. Tracking your progress and reflecting on your mistakes helps keep you motivated. It reminds you of why you started in the first place and encourages consistency. When President Obama addressed students across the country, urging them to work hard and stay consistent, he was acknowledging the same struggles we all face when it comes to perseverance. Life's challenges, like rejection and failure, are the dried-up leaves that fall from the tree of hope. But that tree remains strong, and with the right care and effort, it will sprout new leaves and flowers.

Finally, let's talk about heroes. We all have people in our lives who inspire us. One of the heroes in my life is my grandmother. She was the backbone of our family, always nurturing, always there with wisdom, and a quiet strength that kept us together. Despite her struggles, she remained resilient, and it's that resilience that has stuck with me throughout my life. She never wavered in her love, and her unwavering belief in me has been a guiding light in my darkest moments. Her story of perseverance and grace is something I carry with me every day.

Who is a hero in your life? Why do they stand out to you?

Chapter 5: Failures to Frontiers

Failures are like bumps in the road–blockages that may seem permanent but are only temporary. Imagine you're training for gymnastics to present to the judges on your annual sports day. The first day is filled with failures: you attempt a somersault and fall straight to the ground. These failed attempts are part of a larger process that ultimately leads you to the finals, where you display strength, talent, and the fruits of all your hard work.

Failure is unavoidable. It is ingrained in the process of success. You begin with failure, confusion, and uncertainty, then work toward improvement. Failure is a powerful tool for growth. In every life journey, we need an element of failure to navigate our way to the finished product–success.

To embrace failure, we must first accept it. Some people are insecure about this, and the fear of failure must be eliminated. To achieve anything in life, you must understand that downfalls are inevitable. Failure is not the final destination in your growth journey; rather, it is a bump in the road that you must pass with patience.

Like many others, I once found myself trapped in the cave of failure–a place filled with challenges. To escape, I needed the light of perseverance. I summoned all my mental strength to become the person I am today, proud of the process I committed to. Failures came my way, but I viewed them as bumps in the road that I surpassed without letting them demotivate me.

When failure comes knocking, it's crucial to face it with the courage you've built. Thomas Edison famously said, "I have not failed. I've just discovered 10,000 ways that won't work." Failure isn't just an obstacle; it's a valuable teacher. It provides lessons that illuminate the path to success and how to pursue it with determination.

Failures are not the end but the fuel that drives determination, and this determination, in turn, propels you toward your goals. I've experienced this cycle firsthand throughout my life, and one significant instance was during my sophomore year of college, where I found myself in the trenches of my organic chemistry class. The material was complex, the course load overwhelming, and I often felt completely lost, unsure of how I would manage to pull through. It was one of those moments where doubt creeps in and questions your abilities. "Can I really do this? Am I smart enough?" The pressure was immense, and the weight of the challenge felt heavier with each passing week.

But for me, giving up was never an option. I refused to let this single roadblock define the course of my future or stop me from reaching my destination. Despite feeling discouraged, I knew that the only way out was through—so I picked myself up and took a different approach. Instead of wallowing in self-doubt, I decided to dedicate extra hours to my studies. I spent evenings and weekends pouring over textbooks, watching tutorials, and solving problems over and over again until I began to understand the material better. I sought help from tutors who could break down difficult concepts and guide me through the more intricate aspects of organic chemistry. Every day, I worked on practice exercises, repeating formulas and reactions until they became second nature.

Slowly but surely, I emerged from this struggle, and my potential for success became clearer. I didn't magically become an expert overnight, but my persistence paid off. My grades started to improve, and I began to feel more confident in my understanding of the subject. Through determination, hard work, and a refusal to quit, I managed to turn things around.

What this experience taught me is that failure can have a profound impact on your motivation. When faced with setbacks, it's natural to feel defeated and lost in the chaos of your own doubts. However, this is where a strong support system can make all the difference. As I've mentioned earlier in this book, having friends, family, and mentors who are invested in your journey can be a tremendous asset. They can help lift you up when you're feeling low and remind you of your capabilities when you're unsure of yourself.

During my struggle with organic chemistry, I sought help from both peers and professors. At first, I was hesitant to reach out, thinking that admitting I was struggling would somehow make me seem inadequate. But I soon realized that everyone faces challenges, and seeking help is not a sign of weakness but a demonstration of strength. I attended office hours regularly, where my professors helped clarify difficult concepts and pointed me in the right direction. I also formed study groups with my classmates, and we spent hours discussing the material and solving problems together. These study groups became a source of encouragement, as we supported each other through our shared struggles and celebrated our small victories together.

Reaching out for help instead of isolating myself was a turning point. It reminded me that I wasn't alone in my challenges. Others had gone through similar experiences, and their stories helped guide me along my own path. Hearing about their struggles and how they overcame them gave me the motivation to keep going. I found that relating to others and connecting with their experiences can sometimes provide the clarity and perspective you need to navigate your own journey.

When failure strikes, it's important to seek support. Whether from friends, family, teachers, or peers, surrounding yourself with people who care about your progress can make all the difference. Failure can easily erode your motivation, but it doesn't have to. If anything, failure should inspire you to push harder, to try again with more determination than ever before. When faced with challenges, I stayed committed to my goal, refusing to let the difficulty of the subject matter or a low grade derail my focus. I adopted a mindset of positivity, believing that with consistent effort, I could improve and succeed.

Consistency is one of the most critical factors in achieving your goals. Whether in academics, fitness, career, or personal growth, showing up day after day—even when it feels like you're making no progress—is what eventually leads to success. Think about a gym fanatic who can lift heavy weights effortlessly. They didn't start that way. They started small, failed many times, dealt with injuries and setbacks, and yet kept going. Slowly, their strength increased, and they reached their fitness goals. Similarly, learning from failures and staying consistent can transform any challenge into a stepping stone toward your ultimate success.

Failure has also taught me to be patient with myself. We often want instant results, but life doesn't work that way. Sometimes, it takes time to learn, to grow, and to overcome obstacles. I learned that setbacks aren't indicators of my limitations but opportunities to reassess my approach. With determination, even the most daunting challenges can be overcome. I came to understand that failure is not a final destination—it's merely a part of the journey, a step closer to achieving my goal.

When you encounter failure, you have a choice: give up, start over, or take a different approach. In most cases, the last option is the most beneficial, as it offers clarity and insight. Failure helps you understand your weaknesses and identify the factors that contribute to your success. Use these lessons to guide your future efforts and avoid repeating the same mistakes.

In my case, after my initial struggles with organic chemistry, I decided to approach the course from a different angle. Instead of relying solely on lectures, I added more self-study sessions and created a structured schedule that allowed me to stay on top of the material. I surrounded myself with people who could support me, maintained a persistent attitude, and didn't let discouraging words or low grades get in the way of my progress.

Through determination, consistency, and a strong support system, I eventually succeeded. I realized that failure wasn't something to fear,

but something to learn from. It fueled my determination and pushed
me toward my goals. And now, I know that no matter what challenges
lie ahead, I have the tools and resilience to face them head-on and keep
climbing my Everest.

This experience shaped my approach to future struggles and helped
me realize my potential. I understood that giving up was one option, but
pushing through allowed me to discover abilities I hadn't known I had.
If you don't believe you can do something, do it anyway. You'll unlock
potential that can either propel you toward your current goal or guide
you toward a new one that better aligns with your desires.

Perseverance teaches patience and kindness—especially kindness
toward yourself. It also provides the strength to overcome daunting
challenges.

Struggling in school, as I did, can be disheartening, but in the end,
it can transform you. Learning from setbacks and adjusting your study
habits can set you on the right path–a path that not only helps you
achieve your current goals but also benefits your future endeavors.

When you fail, take time to reflect. To truly understand the problem,
you need to analyze the situation and identify where things went wrong.
In my case, it was the amount of time I was dedicating to studying. I
needed more time and guidance from my teachers to get back on track.
Failure offers the perfect opportunity to pause, look back, and dissect the
issues.

The next step is to cultivate a growth mindset. When you fail, you
can surpass that obstacle by continuing to push through the challenges.
This mindset fuels your love for learning and helps you better understand
not only yourself but also the nature of your goals. Viewing failure as a
step towards growth rather than a setback keeps you moving in the right
direction. Failure might close one door, but it opens many others.

When I struggled with organic chemistry, I didn't just seek help
from my teachers–I also asked for feedback. Feedback, no matter how
small the progress, can pull you out of a slump. It motivates you to stay

consistent and aim for better results. Constructive feedback is essential for moving your goals in the right direction. You may have the right goal, but without the proper tools, you risk spiraling into failure again and again. That's why having the right resources is crucial for growth.

At the beginning of this book, I quoted a rather cheesy phrase often used when dealing with failure: *"If at first you don't succeed, try again!"* Although it sounds cliché, when expressed more thoughtfully, it can truly inspire those facing struggles.

I've got a long list of failures. I'm a college dropout–I didn't finish my BA/MBA/DHA until 15-17 years after I left school. I've had relationship failures, financial setbacks, and even personal health struggles. But one thing remains constant: **I NEVER GAVE UP.** As long as you are alive, there is always an opportunity to persevere and make meaningful changes.

Now, reflect on your own experiences. What are some failures you've faced, and what lessons have you learned moving forward?

Chapter 6: Summiting Your Everest

Dreamers.

What is the ultimate goal of big dreamers? Skeptics might discourage them, but they continue to persevere in their ambitions. They fixate on their dreams and do their best to achieve them.

Life is a never-ending series of challenges. From the moment we wake up, we are constantly bombarded with issues, big and small, that demand our attention. Amid all these struggles, we keep pushing forward, working tirelessly toward our goals. Whether we're trying to be successful in our careers, get good grades, find love, maintain good health, or achieve personal fulfillment, we all have something we're striving for. The road is tough, the obstacles are relentless, but we keep going, driven by the hope that our dreams are worth the effort.

These dreams, the things we imagine and aspire to, don't just vanish. They live on within us, sometimes quietly in the background, sometimes burning brightly at the forefront of our minds. But the truth is, our dreams need more than just imagination to survive—they need action. They require consistent effort, discipline, and persistence to bring them to life and connect them to our reality.

Imagine your dreams resting at the peak of Mount Everest, towering over the world, surrounded by clouds and glaciers. They are there, waiting for you, longing to be achieved. But to reach them, you must begin your climb. You must battle the biting cold, the thinning air, and the treacherous terrain. Your dreams want to witness your happiness, but they demand that you fight for them, that you earn them.

Like everyone else, I had dreams and aspirations, too. As I approached the end of my college journey, I envisioned the next stage of my life filled with triumph and success. After struggling for 24 long years, I was ready to become someone. I wanted to be influential, someone with an important message to share with the world. I wanted people to listen to me, to learn from my experiences, and to gain something valuable that would help them live better lives. More than anything, I wanted to inspire others. I wanted to be a source of light, a guiding force for those who, like me, had faced adversity.

I remember clearly the feeling of excitement and ambition that accompanied me as I walked across the graduation stage. Picture a bright-eyed college graduate stepping into the real world, full of hope and energy, ready to conquer the corporate world, earn enough to pay off student loans, and finally begin living the life they had worked so hard to prepare for. I believed that with my education and determination, I would be able to overcome any obstacle, build a successful career, and live a life of fulfillment and purpose.

But as I quickly learned, the reality of the world—especially the reality of capitalism—was far different from what I had imagined. The professional world wasn't the smooth path I had envisioned. The climb toward success was steep and treacherous, with no clear road ahead. Early in my career, despite all my dreams and ambitions, I found myself encountering more problems than I had ever anticipated. Every step felt uncertain, like a clumsy toddler learning to walk. Just when I thought I had found my footing, the turbulent winds of life would sweep me off balance again, and I would have to start over.

It felt as if I were climbing my own Everest, struggling to ascend as the icy winds of doubt, failure, and hardship pushed against me. The setbacks seemed endless, and for a time, it felt like I would never reach the summit where my dreams were waiting. I faced one obstacle after another—some personal, some professional—but with each setback, I had a choice: to give up or to keep climbing. Every time, I chose to keep going.

Nevertheless, I persevered.

Each closed door led me in a new direction. While it was intimidating to face the unknown, I refused to let it defeat me. I learned to embrace failure, not as a sign of weakness, but as a necessary part of the journey. I accepted my mistakes, took ownership of my struggles, and embraced everything that came with the process of growth. Even when I couldn't see the light at the end of the tunnel, I kept working hard, driven by the hope that one day, I would witness my dreams becoming reality.

I pushed through every obstacle for the younger version of myself, who had once been lost in the chaos of family disputes and had endured the pain of being bullied in high school. I climbed for my college self, who had worked tirelessly to get by, to earn good grades, and to survive each day. And I continued climbing for my future self, who I knew deserved to see those dreams come true.

Life could have been smooth sailing, but it never was. It bombards you with problems, constantly testing your resilience, but it's through these challenges that we grow stronger. The more I encountered difficulties, the more I learned to adapt, to persevere, and to trust in my ability to overcome. I realized that these setbacks, while painful, were shaping me into the person I needed to become to reach my goals.

In the end, I refused to let anything stand in the way of my dreams. Life tried to knock me down over and over, but I kept getting back up. And with each fall, I became more determined to keep climbing. The journey was never easy, but I discovered that it was the struggle itself that made reaching the top of my Everest all the more rewarding. Every obstacle I overcame, every failure I faced, added another layer of strength and perseverance to my spirit. It was through this journey that I found my true self—not in the destination, but in the climb.

Early in my career, I felt like a contestant on a reality TV show called ***Job Search Survivor***. The challenges were as daunting as finding matching socks in the dark. Rejection emails became a daily dose of disappointment, and failed interviews felt like an endless loop of awkward conversations with strangers who held my future in their hands. It was like trying to dance the Macarena at a wedding without knowing the steps–clumsy, embarrassing, and ultimately futile. I'm sure many of you can relate to these early career struggles.

Instead of throwing in the towel and retreating to my college dorm to binge-watch Netflix forever, I decided to channel my inner Rocky Balboa and fight back. It wasn't easy, but with determination as fierce as a mama bear protecting her cubs, I refused to let setbacks define me or derail my dreams.

There were moments when I felt like giving up and becoming a professional nap-taker. But I kept my end goal in mind. I knew that success was within reach if I continued to push forward with unwavering perseverance.

All those late nights perfecting my resume were crucial steps in my journey. I knew they would pay off, and they did. I defied the odds and overcome numerous hurdles to reach the light.

Struggles and setbacks were a part of my career–and perhaps yours, too–but the result is always beneficial. As mentioned in the previous chapter, problems are like stepping stones. Like Sisyphus, we push the boulder up the mountain every single day, smiling and hoping—hoping for the sake of hope.

My challenges shaped who I am today because I learned from them. My dreams were too precious to let go.

And, like my story, I've come to realize that everyone's dreams are equally precious. Even if you're surrounded by pessimists who try to weigh you down, never back away until you've reached your full potential. You must always discover what you're truly capable of. The mountain of success and dreams is too grand to avoid.

There will be times when giving up feels tempting. It seems easier in the moment–to stop everything, open a taco stand by the beaches of California, and live a life you never imagined for yourself.

But you'd be wrong. The dreams we sculpt in our minds are meant to be fulfilled. They aren't random fever dreams that haunt us at night; they are our aspirations and goals—what we want to achieve in life.

We all encounter challenges. That's perfectly normal. Moving forward requires Grit, resilience, and often, a caffeine-fueled mindset. It also demands sleepless nights, deep contemplation, and perhaps a few mental breakdowns. But every single element that contributes to this process is worth it.

Certain success-promoting elements can be integrated into your routine. The peak may be high, but it's achievable. You need a structured and calculated approach to reach it.

First, be more specific with your goals. Close your eyes and imagine what you want most in life. Then, write down how that goal can be achieved. Once the larger goals are noted, break them down. Make them more specific. From primary goals, derive secondary ones, and from secondary, create sub-goals. Each step, no matter how small, provides clarity.

When mountain climbers strategize, they develop techniques to move forward. A dream without a strategy is like a balloon without a string–dreams need to be held firmly to achieve them.

The achievement of dreams may have a supportive audience, but it's a solo act. It's like embarking on a solo travel adventure that's both intimidating and exciting. At the end of the day, you must remind yourself that **you** are the one climbing the mountain. People may support you, but it's your feet that must reach the peak. For this, not only is a strategy required, but also self-reliance. Confidence plays a crucial role.

Taking leaps of faith is easier said than done. Some might find spontaneity appealing, but even that needs to be navigated. Overanalyzing or being excessively spontaneous can both lead to adverse outcomes. It's wise to balance and integrate both approaches into your process.

Once you've found that balance, devise a plan for the most effective and efficient way to reach the peak. Avoid impatience when creating these plans-they require deadlines and careful consideration of potential obstacles. It's like a climber figuring out how to overcome challenges and harsh weather during their ascent.

Prioritizing your work is also essential. Devising a plan and setting goals is one thing; analyzing and incorporating them into your daily routine is another. This requires careful time management. Make a weekly planner and prioritize tasks accordingly. I always kept this in mind when I needed to complete a task.

Amid all the hustle, self-care is crucial. You must take care of your mental health while working toward your goals. Self-care is just as important as your aspirations, if not more so. By practicing self-care and maintaining perseverance, we feel better about ourselves. Both aspects of life go hand in hand.

Small lifestyle changes that support both your well-being and your goals should be incorporated. Start waking up early, go for runs, meditate, or drink coffee—whatever helps you feel better.

As Michelle Obama said:

"Whether an illness affects your heart, your arm, or your brain, it's still an illness, and there shouldn't be any distinction ... We don't consider taking medication for an ear infection something to be ashamed of. We shouldn't treat mental health conditions any differently."

Climbing your Everest is much like tackling the challenges you experience during travel. Whether you're embarking on a hike or navigating a foreign country, the experience can be both exhilarating and daunting. Success requires careful preparation, attention to detail, and, most importantly, planning.

Traveling alone, much like leading your own life, offers a freeing but challenging experience. It allows you to fully immerse yourself in unfamiliar and exciting environments, discovering new cultures on your terms. However, just as you'd plan an itinerary for a trip, you must also prepare for life's journey. Mapping out goals, understanding the obstacles ahead, and facing them directly are as essential in life as they are in travel.

Once you embark on your journey—whether it's a life goal or an adventure abroad—obstacles are inevitable. Just as you might get lost in a foreign land, you may face unforeseen difficulties in achieving personal goals. But the key in both situations is to stay calm. Keeping a cool head gives you the clarity to navigate your challenges effectively, making them more manageable and less intimidating.

Traveling solo can lead to profound personal growth and valuable lessons that stay with you for a lifetime. Independence and self-reliance are fostered by stepping outside your comfort zone and embracing new experiences. Solo travel encourages cultural awareness and empathy, as you interact with people from different backgrounds and face unique situations. Each challenge you overcome sharpens your ability to adapt, and the personal development from these experiences is priceless.

The lessons learned from navigating life's obstacles mirror those gained through travel. Both are journeys that, at times, push you to your limits but leave you stronger, wiser, and more resilient. Embracing challenges with an open mind can transform both your travels and your life. It's about being adaptable, resourceful, and willing to learn. Open-mindedness, in fact, is one of the most valuable tools for both travel and life. It allows you to face obstacles with flexibility and grace, enabling you to grow and overcome with greater ease.

So, go ahead—open yourself up to challenges and take that leap of faith. The mountain you're climbing may seem insurmountable at times, but you have the strength to reach the summit. It's not just about reaching the top; it's about learning from every step along the way.

I can say this with conviction because I've done it. My path wasn't smooth. I've faced challenges that would make even Hercules break a sweat. But like Superman, I pushed through each obstacle with determination and resilience, refusing to let anything stand in the way of my dreams. There were moments when I stumbled, moments of doubt, but I pressed on with unwavering willpower.

The journey wasn't easy, but that's precisely what made the outcome so rewarding. My career and life were built upon overcoming countless obstacles. Every setback made the eventual victories even sweeter—like winning a marathon after tripping over your own shoelaces halfway through. In the end, it's not just about reaching your destination; it's about appreciating the strength and perseverance it took to get there.

So, as you climb your own mountain, remember: it's the bumps in the road that make the journey worthwhile.

I encourage you to reflect on what you've learned, define your goals, and consider how things will change now that you understand the **Power of Perseverance**.

Don't miss out!

Visit the website below and you can sign up to receive emails whenever Dr. Michael A. Smith publishes a new book. There's no charge and no obligation.

https://books2read.com/r/B-A-CXROC-VDLDF

www.ingramcontent.com/pod-product-compliance
Lightning Source LLC
Chambersburg PA
CBHW051825130726
47987CB00003B/1408